"A beautiful wise and intuitive offering from a wise and well respected leac to those who want to employ intuitive wisdom in their leadership in thes $

—MALCOLM STERN, co-founder of $\cdots$

"Wise, inspiring and beautiful. This unique book presents a new vision of leadership that can help us take the human adventure to the next level."

—TIM FREKE, philosopher and author of 35 books

"A must have that you will want to refer to over and over again. I literally felt my leadership expand and evolve into one of an energetic architect as I was reading this book. Connect to the essence of this beautifully powerful, captivating book and be prepared for your life and work to be forever changed."

—DIANE WILLIAMS, Founder, The Source of Synergy Foundation, Initiator, The Evolutionary Leaders Circle.

"The reset button the leadership world has been waiting for. Any leader embodying his 12 Principles will have the authority, presence, autonomy, and relaxed confidence to inspire meaningful deeper resources in other people."

—RAFIA MORGAN, Therapist and Teacher

"Peter Merry is a master in his field. There are uncountable words printed every year about leadership. Here, Peter offers something different. Images that take the reader beyond words into a symbolic landscape that requires contemplation, self-examination, and deep reflection. A slim volume that will take minutes to read and years to digest."

—DAVID PEARL, author of *Wanderful*

"*Leading from the Field* is an invaluable, empowering, and practical guide for leaders to experience and embody a wholistic world-view."

—DR JUDE CURRIVAN, author of *The Cosmic Hologram* and co-founder of WholeWorld-View

"*Leading from the Field* not only helps to give words and images to the energetic dimensions at play but also guides us in how to pragmatically engage with them."

—TATIANA GLAD, co-founder Impact Hub Amsterdam

"Of all the leadership books I have read, this treasure chest of qualities resonates exquisitely with the core leadership patterns I aspire to live and seek in others."

—MARILYN HAMILTON PhD, Author of *Integral City* Book Series

"A wonderful read... *Leading from the Field* articulates how a conscious, spirited and transformational leader could be in these rapid times of change upon our Planet."

—JARVIS SMITH, co-founder MyGreenPod.com & PEA Awards

"A bedside table gem for daily state-changing inspiration."

—JAN BONHOEFFER MD, Founder Heart-Based Medicine, Author Dare to Care

"*Leading from the Field* captures the essence of productive stewardship and organizational resonance in twelve concise and germane observations, beautifully illustrated with images that encapsulate the essence of each. These principles guide the creative development of all living systems, at all levels, from the microscopic to the Universal."

—BRENDA DUNNE, President of International Consciousness Research Laboratories

"This book is an excellent guide to explore the energetic dimensions of the universe so that we can co-create a peaceful, just and coherent world."

—DR GYORGYI SZABO, Dean of Graduate Studies at Ubiquity University

"*Leading from the Field* offers leaders within any scale of system or organization ready access to twelve essential principles that can profoundly influence both daily and long-term processes for all involved."

—MARSHALL LEFFERTS, author of *Cosmometry*

"Peter Merry has taken leadership into the invisible energetic realms."

—DR. JIM GARRISON, Founder State of the World Forum with Mikhail Gorbachev

"Peter Merry will be guiding us for more than 25 years into the future. *Leading from the Field* helps me to grow in both my job and my passion."

—AART BOS, CEO Masterpeace

"Life's natural laws and inner wisdom are all integrated beautifully here. Peter is a much needed 'wake up' catalyst and visionary."

—ROGER TEMPEST, Custodian, Broughton Hall Estate

Leading from the Field provides the gift of practical and heartfelt wisdom to anchor us into an integrated, intuitive and compassionate form of leadership."

—PARIS ACKRILL, co-founder of Avalon Wellbeing Centre

"Peter Merry's new book shines a light on the qualities humanity needs to explore in order to rebalance ourselves and our global civilization."

—DR. ROBIN WOOD, Author of 8 Award Winning Books

"This exquisitely simple and beautifully produced book reads like a 'Tao of Leadership'."

—DAVID LORIMER, Scientific and Medical Network

Leading from the Field offers 12 powerful principles to complement one half of reality that is about manifest performance statistics, measurable results and expression in the world, with the other half of reality that is about emerging potential, coherence and interrelatedness. Inspiring, practical and highly recommended!"

—HANS ANDEWEG & RIJK BOLS, founders of Center for ECOintention

"We can all lead from this field of unlimited potential. This book and its beautiful images invites our hearts to live from the inside out—connected and aligned with ourselves and our environment. Let's do it!"

—MARIANNE DE JAGER, Change Agent

"A treasure which offers you concrete guidance and ways to practise and evolve as a leader into a beacon of hope."

—ANNE-MARIE VOORHOEVE, cofounder The Hague Center

"Captain Edgar Mitchell said 'It's creativity and intuition that will make the world safe for us.' This book is a beautiful testament to what Dr. Mitchell's epiphany in space revealed to him."

—CLAUDIA WELSS, Chairman Institute of Noetic Sciences

LEADING *from the* FIELD

Twelve Principles for Energetic Stewardship

PETER MERRY, PhD

Original Art by Tyra Corona

For information about this title or to order other books and/or electronic media, contact the publisher:

AMARANTH
PRESS

Amaranth Press
5123 W. 98th St. #1081
Minneapolis, MN 55437
amaranthpress.net
contact@amaranthpress.net

ISBNs
978-0-9980317-9-8 (hardcover)
978-1-953754-03-5 (softcover)
978-1-953754-00-4 (eBook)

Publisher's Cataloging-in-Publication Data
Names: Merry, Peter, 1969- author.
Title: Leading from the field : twelve principles for energetic stewardship / Peter Merry.
Description: Minneapolis : Amaranth Press, 2020.
Identifiers: LCCN 2020946102 (print) | ISBN 978-0-9980317-9-8 (hardcover) | ISBN 978-1-953754-00-4 (ebook)
Subjects: LCSH: Conduct of life. | Human beings. | Humanity. | Mind and body. | Ethics. | Self-actualization (Psychology) | BISAC: BODY, MIND & SPIRIT / Inspiration & Personal Growth. | PHILOSOPHY / Social. | BUSINESS & ECONOMICS / Leadership.
Classification: LCC BJ1533.H9 M47 2020 (print) | LCC BJ1533.H9 (ebook) | DDC 232--dc23.

Cover and Interior design: Kathryn Lloyd
Editing: Shannon Ruhl

First Edition

10 9 8 7 6 5 4 3 2 1

This book is dedicated to Hans Andeweg and Rijk Bols, who have pioneered the field of ECOintention, as well as to those people present and future who embark on this sacred work.

The inspiration and much of the content of this book comes from the writings and work of Hans Andeweg. I have filtered the concepts through my own experience to come up with the twelve principles.

CONTENTS

INTRODUCTION

As we stand on the edge of a new era, with old beliefs, institutions and values crumbling around us, a new realisation is dawning in the minds of many. This is not just an upgrade of our current civilisation. This is a new starting point. From this point on, the foundational assumptions of our civilisation change.

The world we see around us has emerged from assumptions rooted in a belief that what is real is what we can see around us, what we can measure and what we can put a price on. It is rooted in a quest outside of ourselves for the unique distinctive nature of all parts of reality, for definition, naming and control of what we see out there. It is focused on ever increasing growth, progress and expansion, on unlimited possibility in a direction whose only values are about direction and development itself. It is the domain of the mind, abstracted from the apparent limitations of the material and the body.

As such, this movement of humanity on Earth is a sacred expression of life. Life does indeed seek out the sun, growth and blossoming. Yet it is only half of the story. When we base our lives and civilisation on only half of the truth, we are likely to lose our balance. In our desperate search for more, bigger and greater, we have overstretched ourselves, and abused the hospitality of the home and family that make our life possible. We are wobbling precariously, drunk on our own exuberance. We now face a choice—re-integrate the other half of what is true, or topple over in an ugly, painful way into the very muck we ourselves created.

It has not always been this way for us, the human species, this particular offspring of planet Earth. There was a period when our starting point was intrinsic interconnectedness, when time moved in cycles rather than lines, and was inherently related to physical place. We took decisions in consultation with the Earth and other life forms that we share this planet with. Yet in its own way this era also reached a limit, proving too suffocating for the creative expansive self-expressive urge of life that also rages inside of us. So, we embarked on a journey to express that part of life in ourselves. However, in the energy that released we forgot to nurture and reintegrate the values of relationship, belonging and interconnectedness that characterised the previous era. Which is why our unrooted wild expansionism has brought us, and many of the other beautiful species we share this planet with, to the brink of extinction.

I do not believe that the human species is inherently evil and deserves to die because of the pain we have caused to others. I believe we are one of the most creative, beautiful and inspiring expressions of life on this planet. We are just at a particular moment in time where we need to seriously evolve or face the consequences. The laws of nature apply just as much to us as to any other species. Survival of the fittest is not about survival of the strongest, but about survival of those that can fit the best into their context. Our context is the Earth, and our challenge right now is to reintegrate the other half of what is true. To growth, distinction and intellect, we need to add stillness, oneness and intuition.

That is what this small book is about. If we assume, as both the new scientists and ancient wisdom traditions tell us, that all of reality is actually composed of interlocking dynamic energy fields, that life is a continuous process of organising energetic information into form, then what does that mean for the way we need to lead our organisations, be they business, civil society, government, community or even family systems?

We have chosen to use the word "field" to describe the space that exists between things, or out of which things arise. It is our way of pointing to the oneness and inter-relatedness that our ancestors took for granted. "Field" comes originally from the Sanskrit word "prthú" meaning "broad". In its essence we are complementing a hard-focussed view into the separate details of reality with a soft-focussed view of the broad unity of reality. We are not used to looking with soft eyes. We get to see and sense the broad field of reality by accessing our inner worlds of knowing, our intuition. It is not accessible via our cognitive minds, which, by their nature, seek out separation and identification. We have to learn to quiet our analysers and allow the voice of the field to make itself heard in us.

It is from inside that we can learn to perceive, interpret and enhance the energetic fields of the collective systems that we lead. This book is a short beginner's "field guide" to how to go about that. How do we as leaders today learn to steward the energetic dimension of the organisations we are trying to support? When we learn to complement the half of the truth that is about manifest performance statistics, measurable results and expression in the world, with the other half of the truth that is about emerging potential, coherence and interrelatedness, then we unleash the promise of integrating heaven and earth. The forms we create in the physical world will be resonant with the principles of oneness and vitality that exist in the energetic worlds and will serve life in many ways.

As leaders our role will shift from trying to make sure that everything is working increasingly perfectly in the material and relationship worlds, which is impossible anyway, to bridging the energetic, relational and material architectures of our organisations. We need to increasingly direct our attention to the dynamics of the whole, trusting that if the energy is coherent across the system, then the parts will know what to do to be of greatest service to the whole, and will self-organise to do that—just like a healthy body.

In this book, I am assuming that the reader is willing to accept the existence of an energetic dimension to reality, so I am not going to be making the case for that. If you want to convince yourself more of that, you can for example read the publications of Lynne McTaggart, Rupert Sheldrake and the Princeton Engineering Anomalies Research.

My starting assumption is that every living system, everything with a boundary and name—from family to community organisation to department to multinational—has an energetic field associated with it that is continually informing what happens in our visible material world. If that field is not well integrated into the organisation, or carries stressed or blocked energy for example, then the relationships in and around the organisation, and its performance in the world will suffer. As leaders of organisations we have the greatest influence on that field. Through our attention and intention, we enhance or detract from the quality of that field. It is not something we are generally taught in business schools or on leadership courses, yet it carries huge potential for us to co-create organisations that inspire people, serve life and get things done.

This small booklet is designed to be something you can carry around with you, to remind you of some core principles and practices of resonant leadership and energetic stewardship. The principles are distilled from 30 years of work in the field. I experience them as simplicity, the other side of complexity. Allow the words and images on the pages to sink in. The images are original and were created by Tyra Corona through connecting to the essence of each of the principles. Breathe them in, let them resonate with your body, and release your mind to work out what you need to do next to best embody them.

As a leader of organisations myself, I invite you to join me in this inquiry into what I believe is the future of enlightened leadership on our planet today.

The Twelve Principles

BOUNDARIES

Know the boundaries of your leadership.

Know who and what are you accountable for.

Be in authentic relationship with those you are accountable to.

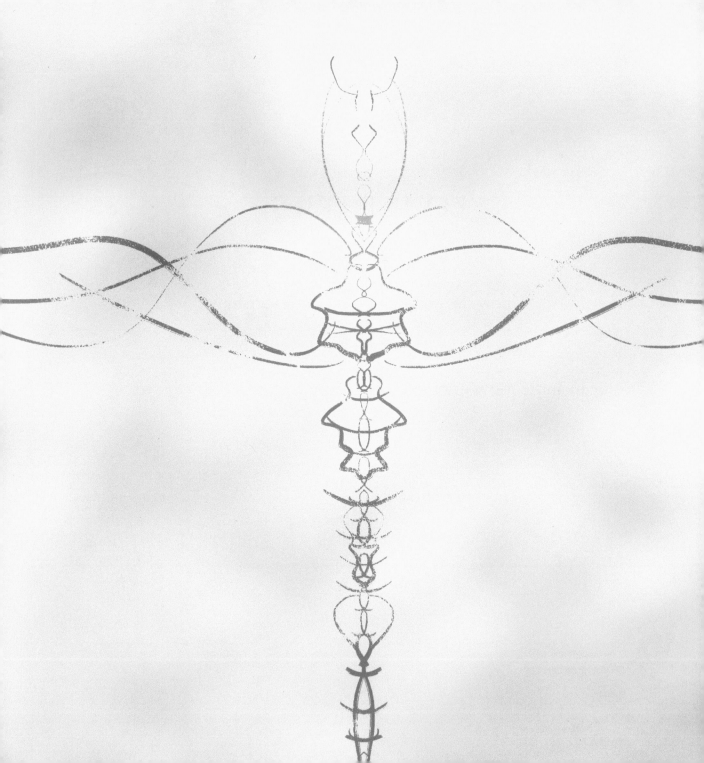

STILLNESS

Be in touch with the stillness in yourself.

From this place you can interact with the energy field

of the system you lead.

ATTENTION

Pay attention to all parts of the system you lead.

Your attention directs the life force.

FEELING

Feel through your heart what is alive in people

and other parts of the system.

Hold it all in the understanding light

of your compassion.

INTENTION

Be clear on your intentions, pay regular attention

to them and visualize their realization.

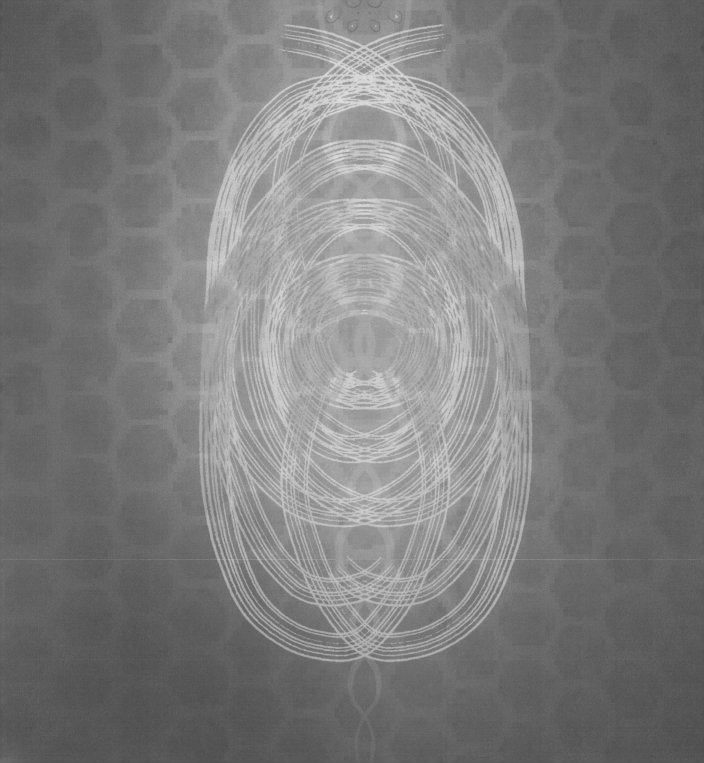

CONTENT

Be actively interested in the content

of what people are working on.

TIMING

Work with the natural rhythms of time.

Go when it flows and stop when it blocks.

PROGRESS

Pay attention to what wants to happen now

and take the next natural step.

That's all.

FORM

Be aware that words, numbers, and geometry form energy.

Be conscious in their use.

PLACE

Always be aware that you are being hosted

by a physical place on the Earth.

Greet each place, ask what it needs,

and treat with respect.

PAIN

Be curious about pain that is held from the past.

Bring it into the light.

Explore what it has to teach for the present.

Embrace and release.

PRESENCE

Enjoy the playfulness of each moment.

Amusement and fondness keep energy moving.

Descriptions

BOUNDARIES

Know the boundaries of your leadership.

Know who and what you are accountable for.

Be in authentic relationship with those you are accountable to.

When you are clear about what you are taking responsibility for, and fully step into that responsibility, the whole system you steward will respond coherently to your intentions.

If neither you nor others really know which pieces fall in your domain, then uncertainty will rule, and responses to your intention will be splintered and half-hearted.

When you have a clear and honest relationship with those you are accountable to, you play a guardianship role for your people, and they can trust your authority.

In times of change, boundaries create groundedness and clarity.

STILLNESS

Be in touch with the stillness in yourself.

From this place you can interact with the field of the system you lead.

When you access the still place inside, you can get a feel for the bigger picture of what is going on. People sense your presence and relax because they feel you are in touch. From that place you can also direct your intentions to the system as a whole and they will start to work for you.

If you are continually caught up in the business of action and activity that takes place outside of yourself, you will get sucked into the huge amount of detail that exists there and lose a feel for the whole. People will sense a vacuum of leadership, stress will grow, and more of the detail will be thrown your way to deal with.

In times of change, stillness puts you in the eye of the storm.

ATTENTION

Pay attention to all parts of the system you lead.

Your attention directs the life force.

If people know that you know they exist, and that you are aware of their role in the whole, they will assume their responsibility. Your attention feeds their motivation and productivity.

If you have blind spots in your awareness of what parts make up the whole of your domain, they will start to wilt like an unwatered flower, and demand attention in all sorts of disturbing ways until they feel seen and included.

In times of change, attention ensures you stay connected to the whole.

FEELING

Feel through your heart what is alive in people and other parts of the system.

Hold it all in the understanding light of your compassion.

If people feel that you care about them, they will warm to you and be loyal to your intentions.

If you come across as cold and distant, people may well do the job as agreed, but you will get little more from them.

In times of change, we need more from people than what is in the job description. We need to feel that we are in it together.

INTENTION

Be clear on your intentions, pay regular attention to them and visualize their realization.

If you are able to picture your desired outcome and recall it regularly, you make it come alive for yourself and others. You and others have a sense of the general direction, and can use it as a compass to guide day-to-day activities, increasing the probability of it manifesting.

If you lack clear intentions or let them drop too far into the background of your awareness, the system and people lose a sense of direction. Activity becomes routine, losing broader meaning, and people start to feel that they are going nowhere.

In times of change, intention has a far greater impact than instability, and draws people and events to it synchronistically.

CONTENT

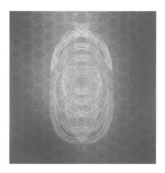

Be actively interested in the content of what people are working on.

If you have some knowledge of what people are working on, people feel that their profession is being seen and included. People have passion for their area of expertise and if you show interest, it will inspire them to share and connect.

If you show no interest in what people are working on, they are unlikely to be interested in you or your opinions. They will work in their own little world and potential synergies will be lost.

In times of change, connections between content areas is critical to seeing and nurturing the emerging order.

TIMING

Work with the natural rhythms of time.

Go when it flows and stop when it blocks.

If you can notice when things are ready to move and when they need more time, it will save you a lot of energy. We can never oversee the whole of reality and there are usually good reasons outside of our awareness why something wants to happen or not.

If you try to force things to fit into your planning, you are likely to create stress for yourself and others and fail to achieve your goals. If the train has not arrived at the station, there is no point in trying to get on.

In times of change, time tends to work less linearly, and we are more effective when we connect to timing more intuitively.

PROGRESS

Pay attention to what wants to happen now and take the next natural step. That's all.

If you can be present to reality as it is now and take the next step that feels like the most natural one to take, you are more likely to be aligned with all the different factors involved. That step may only be one step, but it is taking you towards your goals.

If you try to plan too far ahead and pre-determine which steps to take, you are likely to find that you lose touch with reality. Once you have taken one step, it changes reality, so your plan is already out of date.

In times of change, things move quickly and unpredictably. Staying as close as possible to the present moment is the best way to navigate.

FORM

Be aware that words, numbers, and geometry form energy. Be conscious in their use.

If you are conscious of the way you name things, number things, and structure things, you will notice a significant increase in vitality. Life has natural patterns and proportions which support organic growth.

If you pay no attention to the impact of name, number, and structure, then you increase the chance of creating matches that go against the natural patterns of life. They will drain energy and work against you achieving your goals.

In times of change, the more aligned we are with the natural order, the more effortless the transition is.

PLACE

Always be aware that you are being hosted by a physical place on the Earth.

Greet each place, ask what it needs, and treat it with respect.

If you are conscious of the physical place you locate your activities, you are likely to experience more vitality and supportive synchronicity. A place is loaded with history, geological features, and different energies that influence our experience there. Most of us feel it instantly when we walk into a building. In the East this is more understood, with practices such as Feng Shui.

If you do not pay attention to the location on Earth where you locate yourself and your activities, then you increase the chance of creating misalignments, purely out of ignorance, that could significantly distract from the quality and effectiveness of the work that you do there.

In times of change, one thing we can be sure of is the ground under our feet. Having it work with you or against you can be the difference between breakthrough and breakdown.

PAIN

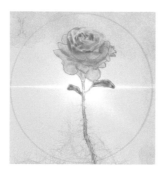

Be curious about pain that is held from the past. Bring it into the light. Explore what it has to teach for the present. Embrace and release.

If you can name, unmask, and engage pain from the past, you will release energy that is stuck to support your project in the present. Past pain normally surfaces at the moment that its energy is needed for the next step, so treat it as a gift.

If you ignore pain from the past, it will keep pulling at you until you acknowledge it. It will find ways to sabotage progress in your project, creating conflict and draining energy. Pain you see in the system you lead is usually related to pain you hold in yourself.

In times of change, the old is being released and the new is being born. As part of that process, old wounds reappear to be healed and integrated.

PRESENCE

Enjoy the playfulness of each moment.

Amusement and fondness keep energy moving.

If you can bring your full presence and playfulness to each moment, then you will notice that creativity and innovation flow effortlessly.

If you are lost in the past or the future, you will miss what is going on right under your nose, which might be just the thing you need to take the next step. If you take yourself or your idea too seriously, you will miss opportunities to evolve even further.

In times of change, nothing is set in stone. A playful attitude keeps you alert and open to rapid change.

RESOURCES

For more information on resonant leadership and energetic stewardship, I recommend:

Andeweg, Hans. *In Resonance with Nature*. Edinburgh: Floris Books, 2009.

Andeweg, Hans. *The Universe Loves a Happy Ending*. Nashville: Turner Publishing Company, 2011.

Institute of Noetic Science: noetic.org

Jahn, Robert & Dunne Brenda. *A Conversation with Jahn and Dunne*. On *The Pear Proposition* [DVD/CD]. Oakland: StripMindMedia, 2005.

László, Ervin. *Science and the Akashic Field: An Integral Theory of Everything*. Vermont: Inner Traditions, 2004.

McTaggart, Lynne. *The Field*. London: HarperCollins, 2001.

Merry, Peter. *Evolutionary Leadership*. Pacific Grove: Integral Publishers, 2009.

Sheldrake, Rupert. *Morphic Resonance: the Nature of Formative Causation* (4th Ed.). Vermont: Park Street Press, 2981.

Talbot, Michael. *The Holographic Universe*. London: HarperCollins Publishers, 1991.

The Center for ECOintention: ecointention.com/index_e.htm

The Intention Experiment: theintentionexperiment.com

The UbiVerse: ubiverse.org

Tyra Corona: SelfAsInstrument.com

Ubiquity University: ubiquityuniversity.org

Volution Theory: volutiontheory.net

Whole World View: wholeworld-view.org

ABOUT THE AUTHOR

Peter Merry is a leader and social entrepreneur who has spent most of his adult life in an ongoing quest for how to be of greatest service to the transition towards a more life-affirming future for people and the planet we inhabit.

On that journey he has been a theatre director and actor, a teacher of English in Paris and northern Ghana, an environmental activist and International Coordinator of the Green Party of England and Wales, a MSc student in Human Ecology, an international youth trainer, co-founder of the business Engage!, an organisational development consultant, public speaker, founder and Chair of the Center for Human Emergence Netherlands, PhD student with and co-founder of Ubiquity University, husband and father of three boys. In the energetic realm, he has trained in clairvoyancy and geomancy, and completed the four-year vocational training in ECOintention. He is the author of Evolutionary Leadership, Volution, Why Work, Leading from the Field, and The Pain and the Promise.

He lives in the ecological neighbourhood Eva Lanxmeer, in Culemborg, the Netherlands, with his Dutch wife and three children.

For more see petermerry.org

The Twelve Principles
Card Cutouts

STILLNESS   BOUNDARIES

FEELING   ATTENTION

CONTENT   INTENTION

PROGRESS   TIMING

51

PLACE   FORM

PRESENCE   PAIN

Other books by Peter Merry:

Why Work?

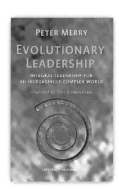

Evolutionary Leadership

CPSIA information can be obtained
at www.ICGtesting.com
Printed in the USA
BVHW051551211221
624588BV00002B/150